WE DRIVE
Fuel Tankers

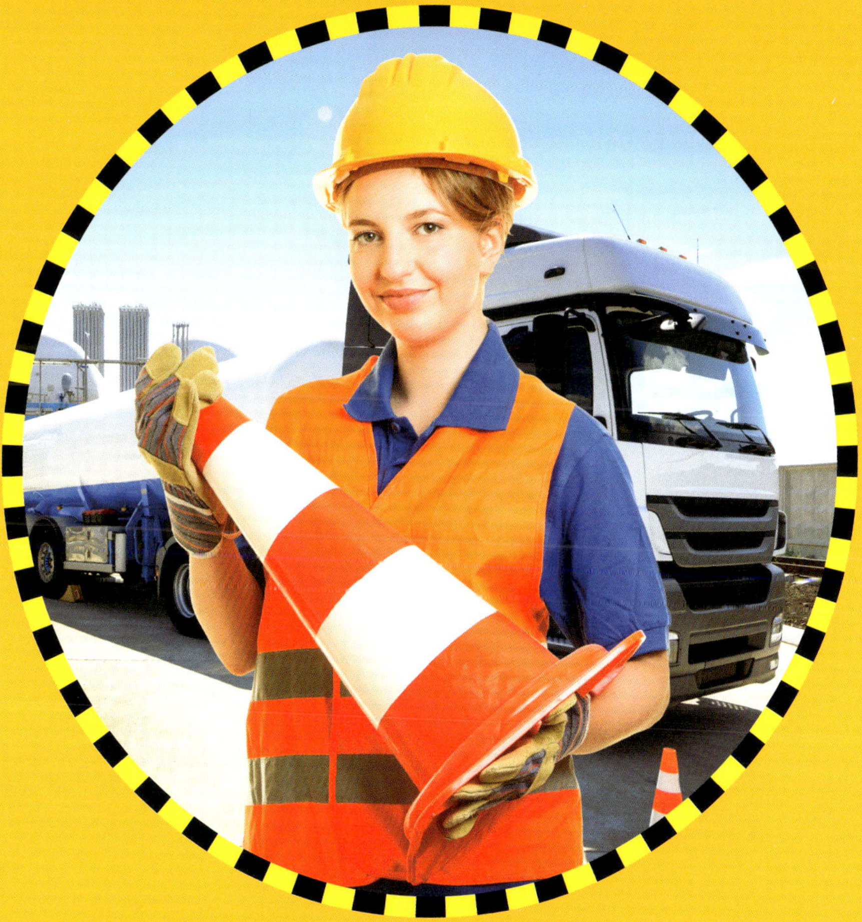

Alix Wood

Ruby Tuesday Books

Published in 2025 by Ruby Tuesday Books Ltd.

Copyright © 2025 Ruby Tuesday Books Ltd.

All rights reserved. No part of this publication may be reproduced in whole or in part, stored in any retrieval system, or transmitted in any form or by any means, electronic, mechanical, photocopying, recording, or otherwise, without written permission from the publisher.

Editors: Ruth Owen & Mark J. Sachner
Design & Production: Alix Wood

Photo credits:
Alamy: 14T (David Bleeker), 14B (Ahmad Faizal Yahya)), 18T (Jochen Tack), 18B (Sheralee Stoll), 19B (Jaromir Chalabala); iStockPhoto: 10T (Ron & Patty Thomas), 14T (ivanastar), 21 (aapsky); Shutterstock: Cover (Tverdokhlib), 1 (frolov_am/Robert Kneschke), 2–3 (Naypong Studio), 4 (f.t. Photographer), 4–5 (Vytautas Kielaitis), 6T (rCarner), 6B (Mechanik), 7T (Miguel Perfectti), 7B (Kalabi Yau), 9 (Fredy Thuerig), 10B (Cobalt S-Elinoi), 11B (GBJSTOCK), 12T (Bogdan Vacarciuc), 13 (2A Stock), 15 (Tverdokhlib), 17T (Chatchawal Phumkaew), 17B (Miguel Perfectti), 19T (Tyler Olson), 20T (Photofex_AUT), 20B (kckate16), 22C (Sanit Fuangnakhon), 22B (WildSnap), 23T (Andromeda Stock), 23B (santypan); Alix Wood: 8, 11T, 13, 16, 22T, 23C.

British Library Cataloguing in Publication Data (CIP) is available for this title.

ISBN 978-1-78856-584-4

Printed in Poland by L&C Printing Group

www.rubytuesdaybooks.com

Contents

Where does our fuel come from? 4

Glossary 22

Index 24

Where does our fuel come from?

We fill our cars with petrol or diesel at a service station.

But how does the **fuel** get there?

A powerful truck with a big tanker delivers the fuel.

Fuel tanker

Wheels

Cab

A fuel tanker truck can carry 400 bathtubs of petrol!

The driver takes their cab to a **fuel depot** to pick up an empty tanker.

A truck in the United States

The driver carefully reverses the cab towards the tanker.

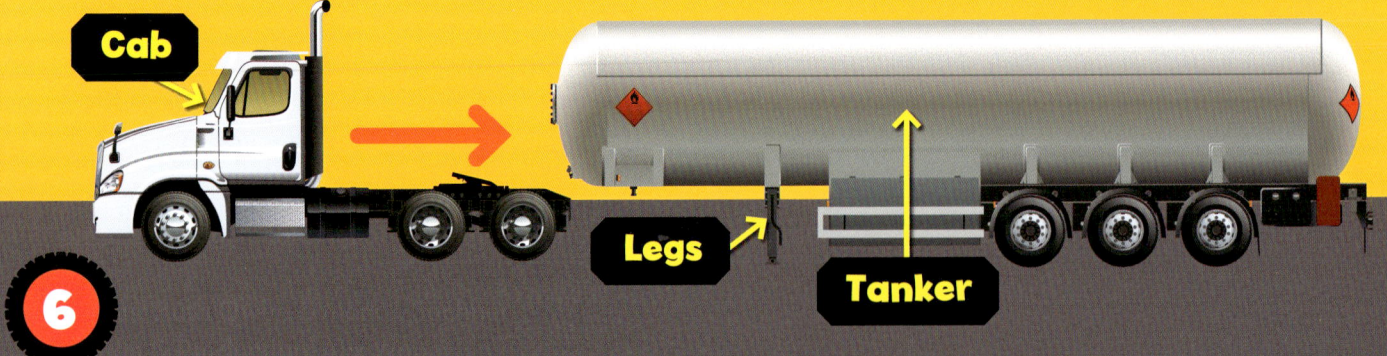

Cab

Legs

Tanker

The driver hitches the cab to the tanker and connects the hoses that work the brakes.

Hoses

A tanker has legs to hold up the front end when it is parked.

The driver lifts the legs with this handle.

Leg

A tanker is split into **compartments**.

The compartments stop the fuel sloshing back and forth.

Compartments

This makes the truck safer to drive and easier to steer.

A tanker can deliver different types of fuel to a service station at the same time.

A tanker may be in an accident.

If the tanker is **damaged**, only a small amount of fuel may leak from one compartment.

Depot fuel tanks

A tanker filling up

Hose

At the fuel depot, the driver fills up the tanker.

Different types of fuel flow through hoses into the tanker compartments.

As fuel flows into a tanker, a dangerous gas called **fuel vapour** is sucked out.

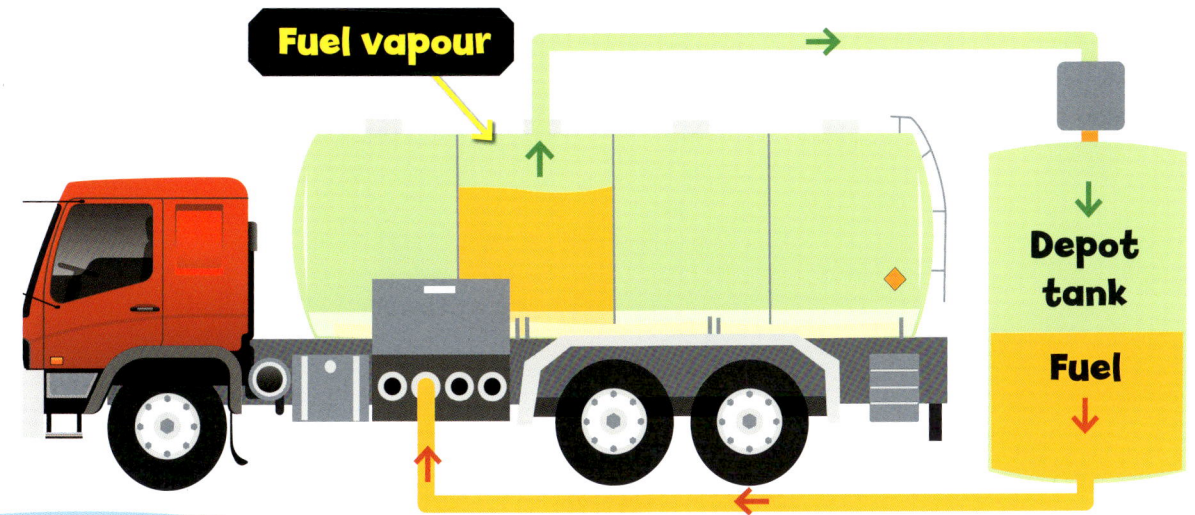

The driver checks the map.

Let's deliver some fuel!

Fuels, such as petrol, can easily catch fire.

A special sign on the truck shows firefighters the truck is carrying petrol.

A driver cleans up small fuel spills with aluminium tools that won't make sparks.

A spark might set the fuel on fire.

Tanker drivers wear safety clothing that protects them from fire.

- Hard hat
- Protective goggles
- Clothes that don't burn
- Aluminium shovel and bucket
- Fire extinguisher
- Boots with metal toes

The tanker truck arrives at the service station.

The service station has big underground tanks.

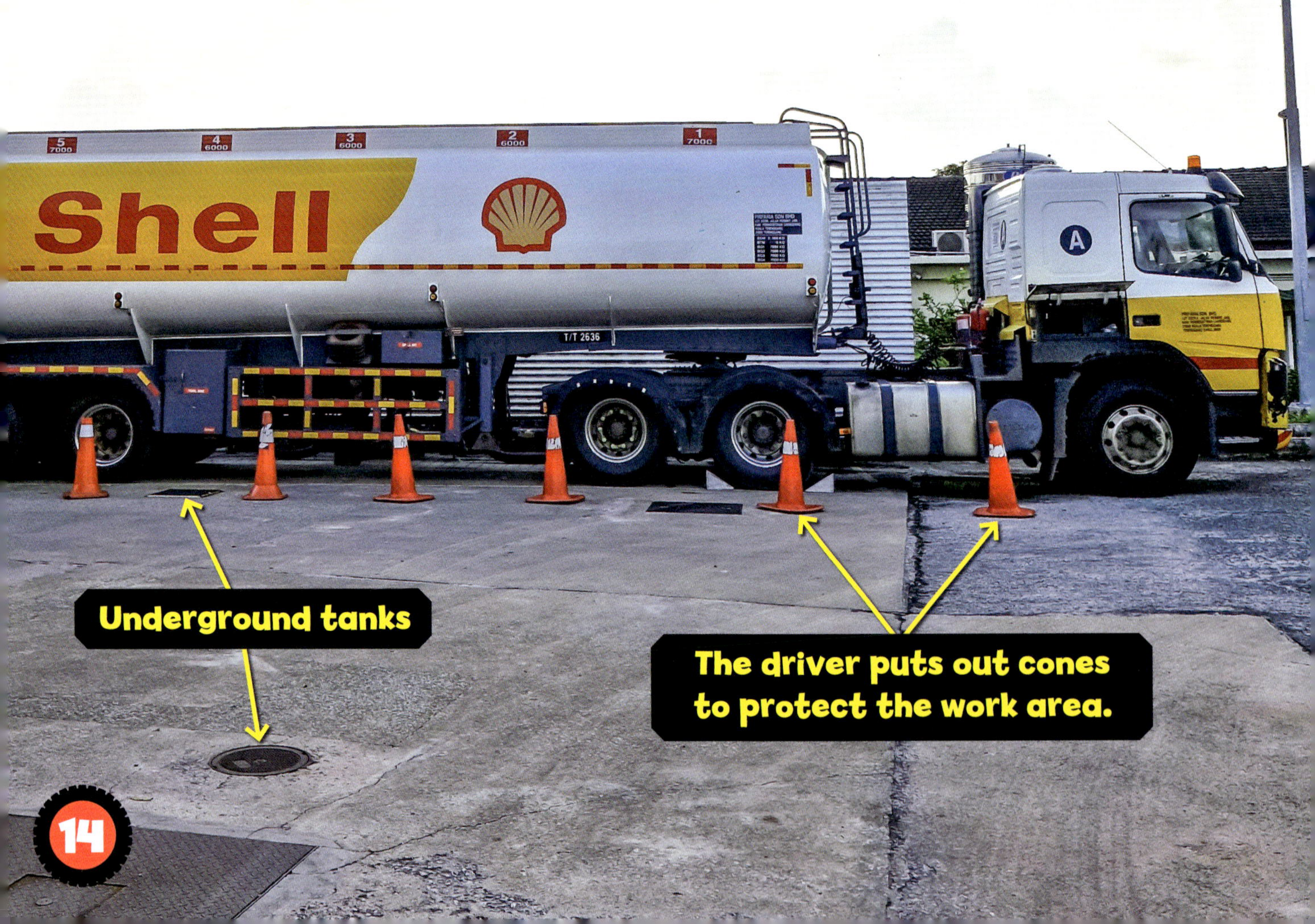

Underground tanks

The driver puts out cones to protect the work area.

The driver attaches the tanker's hoses to pipes that lead to the underground tanks.

Then each hose is connected to the correct tanker compartment.

The driver starts the tanker's **pump**.

Fuel flows down the hose into the underground tank.

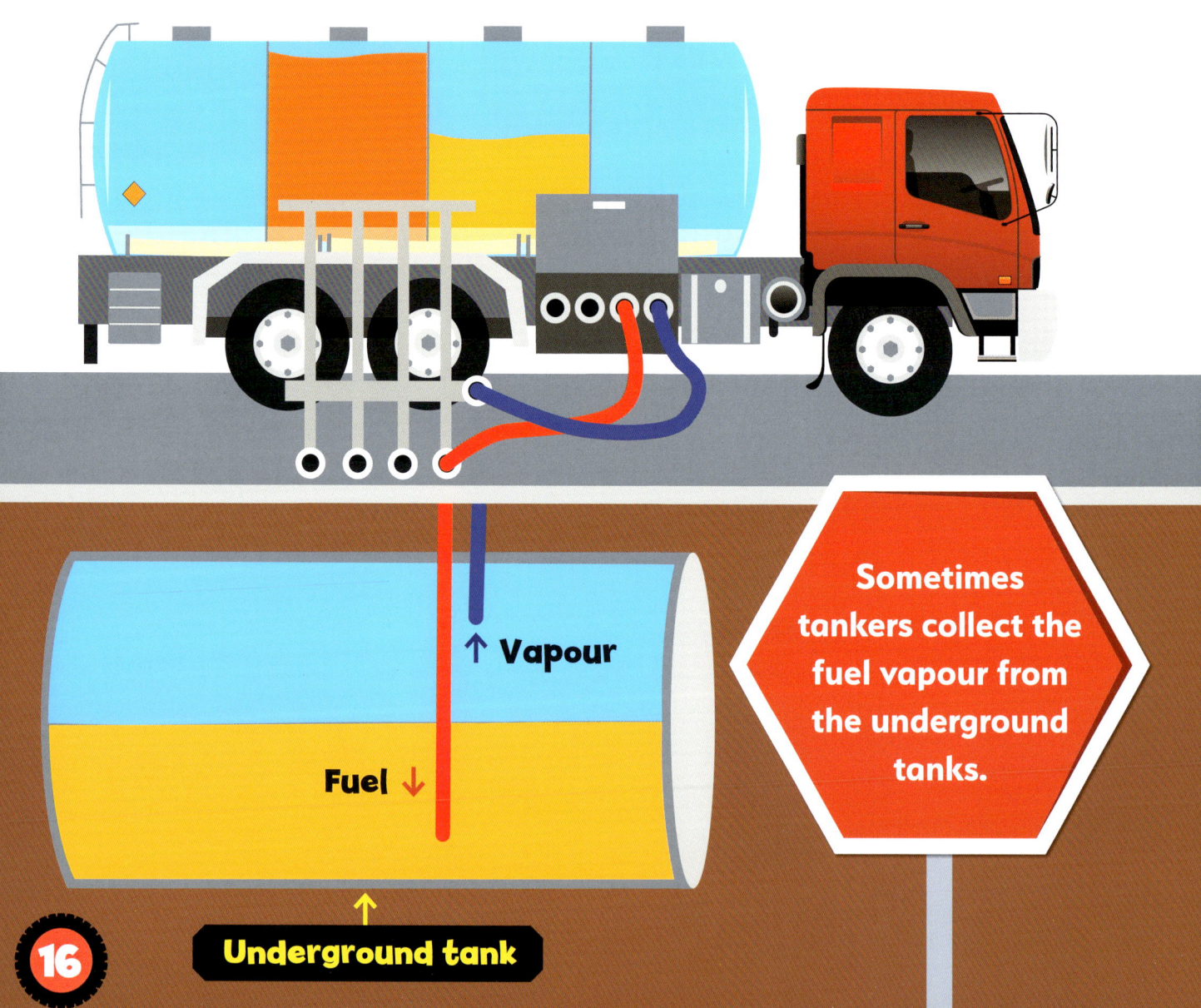

All the fuel has been delivered.

The driver disconnects the hoses and puts them back on the truck.

The driver heads back to the depot.

Another driver is leaving the fuel depot.

This time they have a tanker full of jet fuel!

Jet fuel is a special fuel used by planes.

The plane's fuel tanks are in its wings.

The driver has to climb a ladder to reach.

The driver connects a hose to the plane's tank and fills it with jet fuel.

Some airports have big underground fuel tanks.

A truck connects the underground tank to a plane's wing with a hose.

Some planes park far from the underground tanks.

A fuel tanker must deliver jet fuel to these planes.

An airport fuel tanker

Tanker drivers help planes and cars go on their way!

Glossary

compartment
A separate part of a structure or container.

damaged
Broken or spoiled so a thing no longer works properly.

fuel
A substance such as coal, oil or petrol that is burned to produce heat or power.

fuel depot
A place where large amounts of fuel are stored until they are needed.

fuel vapour
A type of dangerous gas that floats in the air. Fuel vapour can catch fire.

pump
A piece of machinery that moves a liquid from one place to another.

Index

A
accidents 9

C
cabs 5, 6–7

F
fires 12–13
fuel depots 6, 10, 17, 18
fuel tankers 4–5, 6–7, 8–9, 10–11, 14–15, 16–17, 18, 21
fuel vapour 11, 16

J
jet fuel 18–19, 20–21

P
planes 18–19, 20–21

S
safety clothing 13
service stations 4, 8, 14–15, 16

U
underground fuel tanks 14–15, 16, 20–21